Arthur Saliger

THE CATHEDRAL OF
ST. STEPHEN
IN VIENNA

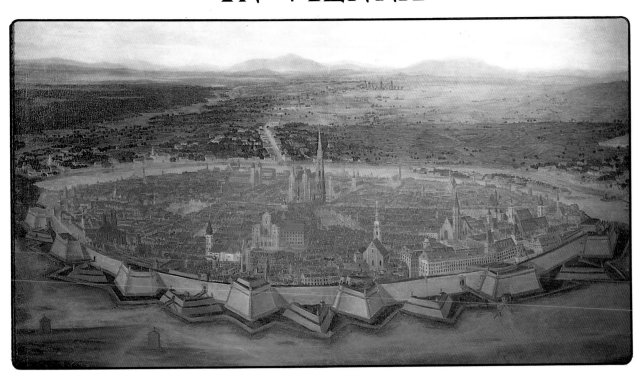

100 Colour illustrations

BONECHI VERLAG STYRIA

CONTENTS

Vertrieb
für Österreich
VERLAG STYRIA
Schönaugasse 64
A-8010 GRAZ
Telex 31-1782
Fax 0316/8063-709

für die Bundesrepublik Deutschland
BUTZON UND BERCKER
Hooge Weg 71 D-4178 Kevelaer 1

© Copyright 1992 by
CASA EDITRICE BONECHI
Via Cairoli 18/b 50131 Florence (Italy)
Telex 571323 CEB Fax 55/5000766

Reproduction even in part forbidden

Printed in Italy by
Centro Stampa Editoriale Bonechi

Translated by Ivor Rowan,
Studio Comunicare

*The photographs are the property of
the Archives of the Casa Editrice
Bonechi and were taken by*
Gianni Dagli Orti

ISBN 3-222-12077-3

View of Vienna

*Domenico Cetto,
oil on canvas, 1690
(Kunsthistorisches Museum, Vienna)*

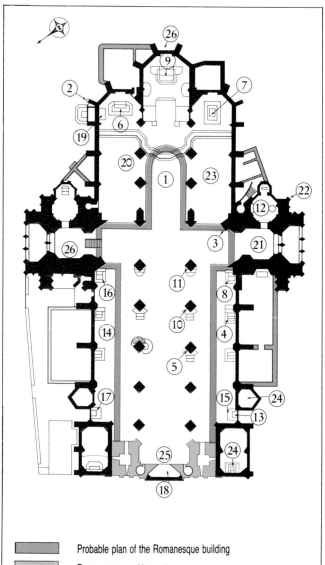

	Probable plan of the Romanesque building
	Romanesque architectonic elements
	Gothic building
	Baroque additions
	Part added in the 19th century

1 Albertine Choir (Women's Choir)
2 Capistrano Pulpit
3 Madonna of the Servants
4 Altar of the Trinity
5 Family Altar or Altar of St. John
6 Women's Altar or Wiener Neustadt Altar
7 Tomb of Frederick III
8 Füchsel Baldachin
9 Main Altar
10 Altar of St. Gennaro
11 Altar of St. Joseph
12 Chapel of St. Catherine (= Baptismal Chapel)
13 Maria Pötsch, Miraculous image
14 Northern lateral nave
15 Oexl Baldachin
16 Altar of St. Peter and St. Paul
17 Puccheim Baldachin (= Altar of the Sacred Heart of Jesus)
18 Giant's Door
19 Tomb of Rudolph IV
20 Altar of St. Francis of Assisi
21 Singertor (Singers' Door)
22 St. Stephen's Tower (= steeple)
23 Southern Choir
24 Altar of St. Valentine (in the chapel of St. Eligius)
25 Western Women's Gallery
26 Christ with Toothache (original in the cathedral, copy outside)

INTRODUCTION

Symbol of Vienna, the Cathedral of St. Stephen still remains the focal point of the city. From an artistic point of view it ranks alongside the cathedrals of Cologne, Freiburg, Regensburg, Prague, Strasbourg and Ulm. Thus it is one of the most important cathedrals in central Europe and may even aspire to pre-eminence over such cathedrals for the sole reason that it was completed many centuries ago, while most of the analogous examples mentioned were brought to completion only in the nineteenth century. This is particularly so in the regions of importance, such as Cologne, Ulm and Prague. St. Stephen's cathedral has got particularly strong links with the Minster of Freiburg (a city that at one time belonged to Austria) and with the cathedral of Strasbourg: at Vienna too, the high tower was constructed contemporaneously with the main building. This tower (familiarly called "Steffl", or "little Stephen"), along with the gigantic roof which unifies the various and disparate elements of the cathedral, synthesises the artistic appeal of Vienna, the vertical axis of the urban ensemble.

However, the unified visual effect of this city emblem should not make us forget the variety of its architectonic background. For the Viennese the sight of the cathedral is so familiar as to be taken for granted, while to outside observers it appears a somewhat unusual architectural creation, at first sight not directly comparable to others. The monumental, yet soaring, tower, with its highly decorative filigree structure, monopolises the attention and often makes the viewer forget that the bell tower is not considered an entity separate from the rest of the building. Yet, aesthetically, its position and imposing nature do make it seem autonomous. The unified visual effect contrasts notably with the heterogenous events that characterize the history of the cathedral: this means that the search for an aesthetic harmony with the pre-existing architectural structures has consistently been present in each of the structural modifications carried out on Vienna's cathedral.

All that remains today of the primitive Romanesque church of St. Stephen, consecrated in 1147 as a parish church in the diocese of Passau, are pieces of the foundations and part of the ground floor in the two western towers and in the atrium of the west portal. What has been definitely established is that this first Romanesque building was only a little smaller than the present one, the outcome of changes in the Gothic style of the fourteenth and fifteenth centuries.

Under the influence of the architectonic design of the Regensburg cathedral, the three-apse enclosure of the pre-existing Romanesque building was widened, creating between 1304 and 1340 a choir of three naves. Apart from possible Westphalian influences (Wiesenkirche in Soest), the Austrian gothic of the thirteenth century was the chief source of inspiration (the Domenican church of Tulln, Lower Austria, no longer standing, and especially the choir in the hall of the Cistercian Abbey of Heiligenkreuz, also in Lower Austria, consecrated in 1295). The desire to create a bishopric in Vienna determined the further Gothic transformation regarding the naves, the two chapels at the sides of the late Romanesque-proto Gothic tribune, and the construction of a high monumental tower, situated on the central axis in front of one of the frontal sides of the Romanesque transept. The plan, which incorporated the late-Romanesque western part and foresaw the two monumental eastern towers, consisted of a Gothic reinterpretation of an architectonic typology which was dominant, in various guises, in the Romanesque imperial cathedrals.

The beginning of construction on the south tower is generally thought to go back to 1359; construction must have started at the same time on the external walls of the nave and on the tribune sides. The plan for a north tower was dropped; the south tower was constructed about 30 metres higher than was planned, because a large belfry was added. The tower, in stone, is 133 metres high (137 metres with the eagle that crowns it) and was completed in 1433. The single levels taper in a closely-packed vertical articulation that rises with gradual scansion forming a reciprocal relationship between structure and decoration, and it is this feature that decisively characterizes this architectonically most refined tower.

The enormous roof was constructed in 1440, in 1446 the nave was covered, around 1450 — as a modification in the plan — the great northern tower was begun, only to be once and for all discontinued in 1511. Between 1556 and 1578 Hans Saphoy constructed the cover of the northern tower, with which the architectural history of the cathedral comes to an end.

In the bombings of the last days of the Second World War the Gothic roof was destroyed (the current roof is a steel construction upon which the Gothic brick ornamentation is reproduced); some of the vaults in the colonnade of the choir also collapsed. Among the items destroyed by a fire were the late-Gothic stalls of the choir, dating from 1476-1486 and a gift of the town councillors, the great cross of Wimpassinger, painted on canvas and seven metres high, the proto-Baroque imperial oratories of 1647 and the Baroque case of the 1724 organ. Thanks to generous contributions from all the Austrian Länder and from the city council of Vienna the reconstruction was swift: in 1952 the inside of the cathedral was completely restructured, between 1954 and 1965 the tower was restored and skillful restorations were successively completed both inside and outside the cathedral.

View from the Cathedral of St. Stephen from the west

This is a view of the cathedral, high above the surrounding houses, and of the tower soaring toward the sky, which was completed in 1433 and called by the Viennese "Steffl" ("little Stephen"). This photograph was taken from the lantern of the cupola of Peterskirche — probably the oldest church in Vienna, now Baroque — and gives a very precise idea of the enormous dimensions of the roof, which is higher than the nave of the cathedral by a height equivalent to five stories: it is precisely for this reason that the late-Romanesque western towers (Heidentürme, or Towers of the Pagans), although 65 metres high, seem very small. This photograph emphasises above all the extremely slanted proportions and the vertical quality of the tower's architectonic elements, as well as the interaction between its finely articulated structure and filigree decoration. It is just this interaction that gives the impression of a progressive upward movement to the tower, which gets gradually thinner all the way to the top. All of the architectural details harmoniously contribute to this upwardly reaching effect, without losing any of their formal qualities. The tower itself is 133 metres high; with the crowning two-headed eagle in metal and the cross it comes to almost 137 metres.

View of the Cathedral of St. Stephen from the Graben ▶

This view of the Cathedral of St. Stephen, the most well-known for 150 years, gives once again the impression of a well-rounded unity and does not bring attention to the "absence" of the choir. One can clearly see that the late-Romanesque western part was incorporated into the Gothic

transformation. The high roof unites the western part both to the chapels, that are of double width in the Gothic style, and to the wall of the nave, rich in windows and extremely decorative with its series of spires. The roof harmonizes all the single architectural elements that originally were quite diverse and also creates a link with the tower, which in this photograph seems to form a perfectly logical crowning to the building, though in reality the Albertine chapel extends to the east of it (that is, to the right and not visible in the photo). It is called Albertine because it was completed during the reign of Albrecht II.

The four towers of the Cathedral of St. Stephen

This photograph, taken from the roof of the archbishop's palace, highlights an often overlooked feature: like the imperial Romanesque cathedrals, the cathedral of St. Stephen also has four towers, despite the fact that this is not obvious to the observer. Rudolf IV of Hapsburg — mindful of the fact that Rudolf I, the first Hapsburg to ascend to the throne, was buried in Spires cathedral — may have proceeded with the Gothic transformation not following the model of the French cathedrals, but according to that of the imperial German cathedrals, even though from a stylistic point of view there are close links with the construction of St. Vitus' cathedral in Prague, which was inspired by French religious architecture.

Tympanum of the Singertor (Singers' Door)

This portal of the nave, constructed between 1359 and 1365, unique in the history of art, has been protected since about 1440 by a polygonal portico. The sequence of Saul's conversion, depicted on the lower part (from left to right: Saul walking towards Damascus, the fall from the horse and the conversion with apparition of Jesus, Ananias placing his hand on the head of the kneeling Saul, giving him his sight back) is very expressive, rich in movement and has an extraordinary spatial effect. The relief, sculpted in a single block of stone, is one of the most splendid examples of the artistic production of the epoch. In the upper part the baptism and martyrship of St. Paul are depicted.

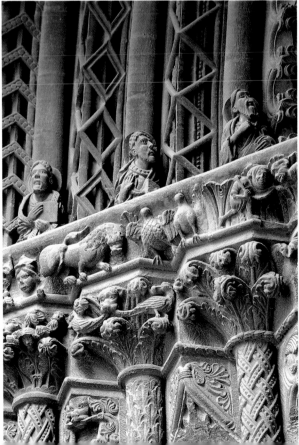

Sculptures in the embrasure
of the Giants' Door.

Singertor: Catherine of Luxembourg, wife of Duke Rudolf IV, with servant carrying coat of arms

In the place of the figures that one would expect to find in the embrasure of a portal, such as characters from sacred scripture or saints, in the Singertor we find the founders of the cathedral depicted. Already for half a century, by that time, the Hapsburgs had made a tradition of depicting themselves as the reigning dynasty. This tradition extended itself to the exteriors also and to the portals: the aim was not only to celebrate themselves but also to express a role of service.

◄ **Sculptures in the embrasure of the late-Romanesque Riesentor (Giants' Door), on the west side**

In the decorative richness of this portal we see the late-Romanesque ornamental art of the Hohenstaufen era reflected; the structure of the capitals, in their projecting shapes, already signals the arrival of Gothicism. The frieze between the capitals and the beginning of the arches show, in the traditional manner of the time, floral motifs enriched with imaginary beings. The busts of the Apostles are turned toward the relief of Christ on the throne, an image of the Last Judgement.

Singertor: Duke Rudolf IV of Austria, known as the Founder, with servant carrying coat of arms

Like his wife Catherine of Luxembourg (daughter of the emperor Charles IV), the duke too is depicted, almost in full tondo, with his heraldic insignia. His role as founder of the cathedral is testified by the model which he holds in his right hand.

Interior of the central nave: view from the choir towards the tribune of the organ; view from the tribune towards the choir

The manner in which the pilasters (against which we find altars and statues under baldachins) join up to the vaults creates the visual effect of a series of large portals.

The homogeneity of artistic conception throughout the various phases of the architectural history — the choir was constructed between 1304 and 1340, the nave between 1359 and about 1440 — is expressed in the relationship between the most ancient construction phases and the most recent, even if in the nave the richness of form characteristic of the late-Gothic and the spreading out of the details is set off in a

highly distinctive manner. ▶
At the point from which the photograph was taken, with a view towards the tribune of the organ, the Baroque altars set against the pilasters are not visible. The other photograph, which has a view towards the choir, shows the discretion of the successive arrangements, even in the liberal dispersion of the specific features from more and more recent epochs.

Historical views of the interior of St. Stephen's Cathedral

Melchior Seltsam:
view from the choir towards the nave and the tribune of the organ (engraving, 1816, Kunsthistorisches Museum, Vienna).
We can make out the funereal insignia — removed a short time later — of the tomb of the emperor Frederick III in the Cathedral of St. Stephen, dating back to the end of the Gothic period and today preserved in the Kunsthistorisches Museum of Vienna. We can also see the baldachin then over the pulpit (today it is over the baptismal font of the cathedral), and in the tribune the casing of the Baroque organ.

The central nave of the cathedral (oil on canvas, signed "LB" and dated 1647, Kunsthistorisches Museum, Vienna). This is the oldest interior view of the church and is in the tradition of Dutch paintings of church interiors. It shows how the cathedral looked at the completion of the main altar in the early Baroque period and other altars of the same era, today replaced with altars from the middle and late baroque; there is also a Gothic altar and a late-Gothic organ over the Füchsel baldachin (the painting is to be found in the Dom- und Diözesanmuseum).

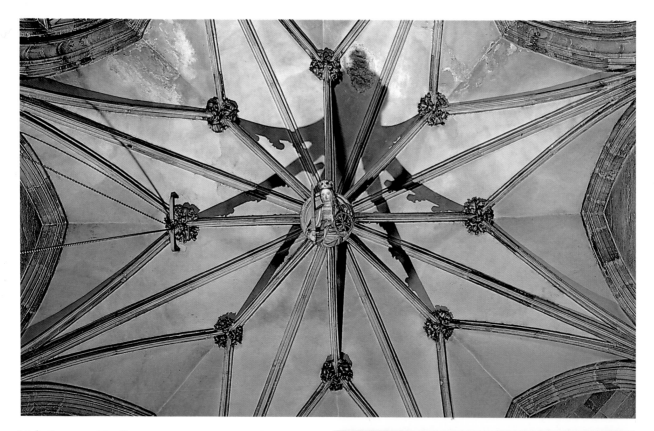

14th Century Vault

To the east of the southern tower we find the chapel
of Saint Catherine, in an octagonal design. This chapel,
of notably slanting proportions, is enclosed by a vault
formed of eight ribs from which hangs a keystone, as
in the cathedral of St. Vitus in Prague. On this we find
a relief depicting St. Catherine of Alexandria,
venerated as the patron saint of science. The
patronage of this chapel is connected to the founding
of the University of Vienna on the part of Duke Rudolf
IV. The crown, the wheel, the sword and the book are
the attributes of Saint Catherine, who underwent
torture on the wheel and was decapitated by the
sword.

In the Albertine choir the subdivisions of the pilasters,
made up of quarter-columns, half-columns and three-
quarter columns (which function as pilaster strips or
projections to help support the vault system) and
including mouldings of various shapes, harmonize with
the progression of the ribs of the vault. The arches of
the arcades, because of their larger dimensions and
their richer outline, differentiate themselves from the
arches of the vault which are uniformly delicate and
form the diagonal ribs of the vault grid.

Vault of the naves, circa mid-fifteenth century

The difference, already visible in the choir vault, between the arches of the arcade, the arches of the vault and the diagonal ribs is seen even more clearly in the naves, both in the southern nave (photo on right) and in the lateral nave (photo on left). Here even the figuration of the vault is different in form from that of the choir.

Pilasters of the naves with Baroque altars ▶

Besides having richer outlines, the pilasters of the naves differ from those of the choir because they are bunched and because they have canopies with statues set against them. The altars set against the pilasters, now Baroque (circa 1700, mostly designed by Matthias Steinl), replace the previous Gothic or early- Baroque altars, as we can see from ancient depictions of the interior.

Late-Gothic sculptures and baldachins in the naves

It is often forgotten that the baldachins of the naves contain a cycle of late-Gothic sculptures of a different artistic level, dating back to the second quarter of the fifteenth century. This could be due to the greater importance of the pilaster sculptures in the choir, which are artistic masterpieces created a hundred years previous to that. The statues in the nave — predominantly of stone — often show traces of more ancient versions, with many parts of the original late-Gothic painting still intact.

The Puchheim baldachin; below, the altar of the Sacred Heart with sacred image from 18th Century

Only in the cathedral of Regensburg can we still find a gathering of Gothic altars with baldachins that is as significant as that of the cathedral of Vienna. Of the three altars with baldachins in St. Stephen's that of Puchheim, at the north west corner of the nave, is the oldest and it retains the design it had at its original construction. It is worth mentioning in this regard that the Viennese collection of designs for the planning of art works is by far the largest in the world (today a small part is conserved in the Kunsthistorisches Museum of Vienna and the larger part in the print room of the Academy of Fine Arts, Vienna): its pre-eminence (298 plans) can be judged only by comparing it to the second largest collection in the world, that of Strasbourg, which contains only 28 plans. This baldachin is generally attributed to Hans Puchsbaum. On the left, beside the altar, is the entrance to the funereal chapel of Prince Eugene, the greatest general of Austria, with an artistic Baroque gate in wrought-iron. Next to it is the tomb to the Humanist Cuspiniano (died 1529) on which is written an epitaph to Hans Reichwein; in its relief we can see the transition from Gothic to Renaissance forms.

Corbel of leaves with gargoyle under the Füchsel baldachin

In the elaborate tracing of the corner corbel's fretwork, set against the wall, a gargoyle has been planted with the face of an animal. The intersecting of the forms produces a figurative unity.

◀ The Füchsel baldachin

This baldachin, which rises from the south-eastern corner with the tribune overhanging it, was donated by private patrons (the middle-class family Füchsel) in 1448 and was made only a little later than the Puchheim baldachin, situated in the north-western corner of the nave. The tribune used to hold the very famous organ of St. Stephen, consecrated in 1514. Under the baldachin is a neo-Gothic altar of 1903, dedicated to St. Leopold, patron of the city. This baldachin gives the impression of a massive body upon which the Gothic fretwork has been superimposed, while the Puchheim baldachin has a lightness of structure, as though hovering in the air.

The Oexl baldachin

This baldachin from the early sixteenth century is found in the south-western corner of the nave. Below it is the miraculous image of the Pötschen Madonna (1697), to which the victory of Prince Eugene over the Turks at Zenta was attributed. This icon comes originally from the Hungarian village of Pócs.

Christ receives the crown of thorns

Part of the late-Gothic Passion cycle from about 1460, on the exterior eastern wall of the southern annex to the choir.

Kapistrankanzel (The Capistrano pulpit), on the exterior north-eastern side of the choir

According to local tradition, Giovanni da Capistrano is supposed to have preached from this pulpit in 1451 against the Turkish invasions and it is because of this that after the victory against the Turks (at Belgrade in 1456) this Baroque apotheosis was constructed. At the saint's feet lie the defeated Turks. Prior to that the pulpit had probably been used for the exposition of relics.

Pulpit

Based on the similarity between the artist's portrait under the stairs of the pulpit (the "onlooker at the window") and the latest portrait of Anton Pilgram of Brünn on the corbel of the cathedral's organ (signed MAP and dated 1513) it is possible to attribute the pulpit also to Anton Pilgram. From a thin stem, encircled by groups under baldachins, the projecting cage of the pulpit develops upward with keel-shaped arches that protrude from the inside outwards, accompanied by sinuous fretwork. These arches visually form the corbel of the pulpit's balustrade,

in which appear other "onlookers at the window", in this case the Four Fathers of the Church that look out from niches in the form of baldachins. The pulpit, Pilgram's most famous work, was probably created in the last decade of the fifteenth century.

◄ The stairs, with its curvilinear progression and its fretworked balustrade, is, in its continuity, of an apparently simple form; in reality it is the result of the complex intersection of four stones, a masterpiece of the rarest sculpting precision.

Above the filigree structure of the foot of the pulpit, which is reminiscent of artistic metalwork, a double crown of keel-shaped projecting arches rises up with a delicate finesse and surrounds the corbel of the pulpit like a basket, giving a chalice-shape to the pulpit as a whole.

◄ Detail of the foot of the pulpit, which demonstrates the energy that was needed to chisel out the stone block and the ethereal quality of the figuration that resulted.

◄ The Fathers of the Church on the balustrade of the pulpit

The Fathers of the Church were theologians to whom four characteristics were attributed: doctrinal orthodoxy, personal saintliness, exceptional scientific capacities and official recognition on the part of the Church. The Church of Rome has proclaimed four since the eighth century: Ambrose, Jerome, Augustine and Gregory I. These four "Onlookers at the window" are also traditionally interpreted as studies in the four physiognomic temperaments that Hippocrates spoke about. From left to right, St. Augustine represents the melancholic temperament, St. Gregory the phlegmatic, St. Jerome the choleric and St. Ambrose the sanguine. Pilgram was particularly adept at rendering the distinct individuality and the vivacity of the different characters.

Anton Pilgram, the "onlooker at the window" at the base of the pulpit

This portrayal shows a younger man to that of the portrait in the corbel of the organ, and thus, as the architectonic style of the pulpit itself confirms, the pulpit can be considered an older work.
The self-portrait of Pilgram, that peeps out from behind the half-closed shutter, conveys the impression of an artist that was aware of his own worth and sure of the success of his work.

Dienstbotenmadonna (Madonna of the servants)

With her sweetly sinuous nature, this Madonna is a sculpture possessing not only a refined grace but also an intense expressiveness in the attention that she gives to the child Jesus, to whom she is united by the veil. The solidity of the figure and the materiality of the treatment of the clothes reminds us that it dates from about 1320/25. This sculpture, one of the most beautiful Madonnas of its time, probably acted as a sacred image for what was at one time the Altar of the Madonna in the Frauenchor (Women's Choir).

Ecce Homo, known as "Christ with toothache"

One of the numerous statues depicting the Ecce Homo on the exterior of the cathedral is this half figure of Christ showing his wounds. It dates back to 1420/30 and the original is now exhibited in the northern tower.

◄ Corbel of the organ

Above the "window" from which Anton Pilgram looks out, complete with square and compass, a corbel rises formed from irregularly arranged hexagons. Above this, ribs develop which embrace from below, like petals, the projecting tribune of the organ. The bust still retains ample amounts of its original colour and shows the master kneeling, with his facial features drawn.
The inscription on the scroll below the window carries the monogram MAP (Meister Anton Pilgram) and the year (1513).

Internal view of the northern lateral nave

This nave, considered independently, can be seen as an autonomous setting, with a longitudinal axis. The subdivision of the walls and the formation of the vault are in total harmony with the nave of the choir in the background (the Frauenchor). With respect to the choir, the naves of the central body have a greater number of ribs in the vault and richer outlines, as well as a decorative variety seen in the baldachins, the pilasters, and so on. At the end stands the altar of Wiener Neustadt. On its left is the tomb of Duke Rudolf IV and his wife Catharine of Luxembourg.

Internal view of the southern choir

With the creation by Niclaes Gergaert from Leyden of the gigantic tomb for the emperor Frederick III, the nave of the southern choir, that typologically is reminiscent of the Palatine Chapels such as the Sainte Chapelle of Paris, acted as an autonomous burial church. The Sainte Chapelle, with its "greenhouse" aspect, strongly influenced the choir architecture of the Central European Gothic churches. One dynamic effect comes from the fact that the various ribs of the vault are of the same type, while the arcades present more accentuated outlines. The inventiveness of the fretwork figuration stands out in the window that shuts in the choir.

Wiener Neustadt altar — Daily side (closed) and Sunday side (open)

This altar, with the late-Gothic transformable front of four panels, was constructed for the new monastery of Wiener Neustadt using pre-existing parts. The predella carries the date 1447. It has been in St. Stephen's since 1883 and was placed in the Frauenchor in 1952. A series of saints are depicted against a dark background in the completely closed position (daily side, see left) and divided into four sections; there is a series of saints on a gold background (Sunday side, see below) in the semi-open position. In all, both inside and outside, there are some 72 figures of saints, three per section. Despite this regular arrangement, thanks to the variety in the representation of the characters and in the fixed and landscape elements, the images never become in any way monotonous.

Wiener Neustadt altar — Sunday side open on particular festivals

In the lower part of the cabinet we find the Madonna with Child with the saints Barbara and Catherine at her side, who are formally still linked with the international Gothic and thus can hardly be dated after 1420; in the upper part the Coronation of Mary grouping beside the Most Holy Trinity could date back to about 1430. The reliefs on the upper left (Coronation of Mary), upper right (death of Mary) and lower right (Adoration of the Magi) could date from around 1420, while the relief on the lower left (Birth of Christ) could be from about 1430.

The Wiener Neustadt altar is without doubt the most important altar in the cathedral of St. Stephen.

Devotional images on the Women's Altar

This devotional image of about 1470/80 comes originally from a Gothic altar — or from a tomb — and was transferred around 1700 to the Women's Altar. At the feet of the Madonna, who is being crowned by angels, we see the kneeling family of the donors. On the left the husband with two children, on the right the two wives, the first with three children, the second with four. Here we see the heavenly and terrestrial dimensions given the respective proportions attributed to them by the people of the Middle Ages.

St. Valentine's altar in the chapel of St. Eligius

The chapel of St. Eligius, dating back to 1360, contains the altar of St. Valentine, from 1500. In the cabinet three statues of saints are arranged in the traditional manner: St. Valentine, St. Ottilia and St. Barbara. At the feet of St. Valentine can be seen the expressive head of a cripple. Above, in the altar-piece, there is a statue of the Ecce Homo under a baldachin.

Altars of Saint Peter and Saint Paul

Beside the corbel of the organ, above a Gothic mensa, the 1677 wooden altar appears. The altar-piece depicts the two principal apostles. On the left there is a statue of St. Leopold, on the right one of St. Henry II.

Main altar ▶

The present-day main altar, built in 1647 by Jakob Pock (architecture and sculpture) and by Tobias Pock (painting), shows the stoning of St. Stephen in front of the walls of Jerusalem. To the sides of this altar-piece are the two national patron saints, Leopold and Florian (on the inside left and right), and the two patron saints of the plague Sebastian and Rocho (on the outside left and right).

Altar of St. Gennaro

Although faithful to its own stylistic principles this Baroque altar adapts itself skilfully to the late-Gothic pilasters of the arcade. The design is by Matthias Steinl and the altar-piece depicts St. Gennaro in the Gulf of Naples by Martino Altomonte. The statues are: on the left St. Charles Borromeo, on the right St. Nicholas. Gennaro was the bishop of Naples and is famous for the miracle of the liquefaction of the blood, spoken of since 1389.

Family altar or altar of St. John

The inventiveness of Matthias Steinl is again seen clearly in the architecture of this altar. Here we can once more admire his capacity to adapt the design and the structure to the late-Gothic pilasters of the arcade. The altar-piece, depicting the family of Mary, is the work of Johann Michael Rottmayr (1708).

Altar of St. Francis of Assisi

The design is by Matthias Steinl, the altar-piece — St. Francis receiving the stigmata — is by Johann Michael Rottmayr (1715). The altar-piece draws backward to achieve an effect of perspective. In the painting at the top is St. Ursula, surrounded by pious women. On the left is St. Virgil and on the right St. Cassian.

Altar of the Trinity

It dates from 1740, from a design probably by Georg Raphael Donner; the altar-piece is by Michelangelo Unterberger, a professor of the Academy of Fine Arts of Vienna. At the centre of the frame there is an open book with the words "In tres unum sunt".

Altar of Saint Joseph ▶

St. Joseph is depicted with the child Jesus in his arms. The design for the altar is by Matthias Steinl, the altar-piece is by Anton Schoonjans, a nomadic painter of Antwerp. Steinl had the title of "imperial engraver" and was an artist of multiple talents: he also worked as an engraver of ivory, a sculptor, an architect, a goldsmith, an artist in stucco and iron.

Tomb of Rudolf IV

This tomb of Duke Rudolf IV the Founder and his wife Catherine of Luxembourg was originally to be found in the centre of the southern nave of the choir, near the descent to the ducal crypt. It was constructed around 1360, in 1647 it was moved laterally in the choir and since 1952 it has been right by the Wiener Neustadt altar. In the niches at one time there were funereal statues depicting the professors of the University of Vienna, founded by Rudolf IV. The two statues, in sandstone, lie alongside each other, in the manner of late-Gothic paintings in which betrothed couples were depicted; the statues would originally have been gold-plated and covered, at least in part, by precious stones. As often happened in Medieval times, the Founder commissioned the tomb while he was still alive.

Rudolf got married at the age of fourteen to the eleventh daughter of the emperor Charles IV. At nineteen he became ruler of Austria and died at a mere twenty- six.

Catherine survived him by another thirty years.

Tomb of Emperor Frederick III

This masterpiece of funereal late-Gothic art is one of the most beautiful works by Niclaes Gerhaert von Leyden, the most important Dutch sculptor of his day, whose works had a notable influence on European sculpture of the second half of the fifteenth century. He began the tomb in 1469, but died without finishing it, probably in 1471. However, the sculptural figuration of the tomb,

not including the lateral reliefs, had already been to a large extent worked on by him or by others under his supervision. The balustrade that runs all round it served as a "catwalk" for the rites of incensation. In the pillars of the balustrade are depicted Christ and the twelve apostles (an allusion to the return of Christ at the Last Judgement), in the arcades are the family saints of the Hapsburgs. On the pillars of the sarcophagus are represented — in the tradition of

the wake — idealised ancestors as representatives of the princedom, while the reliefs show the donations of the emperor to the church. On the cornice are depicted — in the tradition of figuration on tombs — the representatives of the religious and civil institutions, while on the lid is the full-figure portrait of the emperor in gala dress, surrounded by his insignia and the symbols of power.

41

Lid of the sarcophagus of Frederick III

The pictorial conceptions of the Flemish portrait painting of Jan Van Eyck are here transferred to the level of sculpture: the face expresses a quiet absorption, in contrast the clothes and ornaments are full of life. The lid weighs approximately 8700 kilograms. It is in red marble from Adnet and was transported to Vienna in 1479 by river, to be then moved to Wiener Neustadt for work to begin. In order to do this the gun-carriage of an enormous cannon had to be borrowed from the city of Krems; the bridges over the moat surrounding Vienna had to be reinforced and the streets to be suitably adapted. The marble of Adnet, a small town near Salzburg, has been famous since Roman times and is exported world-wide.

Corner pillars of the balustrade of Frederick III's tomb (left), corner pillars of the sarcophagus (right).

Here is the balustrade of the tomb of Frederick III with mortuary symbols on the plinth of the sarcophagus (left) and the physiognomy of an apostle-pillar from the same monument (right), which because of their artistic conception and level of expertise can only be the work of a Master.

Tombs

The tomb of Johann Kechmann, to the right of the entrance to the chapel of St. Eligius, has, on the lower part, a relief from 1510 depicting a month's mind or Gregorian mass (named after Pope Gregory the Great), which was celebrated for the dead person thirty days after his or her death (top left). The upper part is from a slightly more recent era (circa 1515-1520).

The tomb of the Viennese citizen Andre Feder, dated 1510, which is found in the chapel of St. Eligius (upper right).

The tomb of Konrad Celtes, 1508, friend of Albrecht Dürer and professor at the University of Vienna (bottom). At the centre of the laurel wreath is the world *Vivo*. From the formal point of view we see here the end of Medieval devotion. It is attributed to the "builder of tombs to his Royal Imperial Majesty" Michael Tichter, who worked on the tomb of Frederick III.

Even the tombs that were not commissioned by the court show a high level of quality and are of socio-cultural interest, although they do not reach the artistic level of the imperial and ducal monuments. In the early fifteenth century the shrine relief type of tomb was developed, which predominated for a long time: a central figure is depicted inside a cornice in the form of a small temple. The imaginative variety of such shrine cornices is quite striking.

Funereal slab for the bishop Georg Slatkonia, effectively the first ruling bishop of Vienna, founder of the still-surviving institute of the Wiener Sängerknaben, the Young Singers of Vienna (top left). It is an extremely well-moulded and expressive piece of sculpture, attributed to the famous sculptor Loy Hering.

In the chapel of St. Eligius we find the tomb of the canon and professor Johann Kaltenmarckter (top right). On the left, under the cross, is St. Jerome with the lion, on the right is Kaltenmarckter with his two patrons: John the Evangelist (with chalice) and, on the right, John the Baptist.

The funereal slab of bishop Faber displays a certain similarity to that of bishop Slatkonia, but is much less expertly moulded (bottom right).

The tomb of Cuspiniano from 1529. The Humanist Cuspiniano was a confidant of the emperor Maximilian I, special envoy to Hungary, Bohemia and Poland, scholar and rector of the University of Vienna (top).

Baroque tomb from the seventeenth century (bottom left).

Tomb of Prince Eugene of Savoy, the great liberator from the Turks, in the chapel of Tirna, 1736 (bottom right).

Baptismal font in the chapel of St. Catherine

This marble baptismal font from Salzburg has the Four Evangelists on the base and in the shallow niches of the basin are Christ the Saviour, the twelve Apostles and the patron saint of the church, St. Stephen. It was made in 1481 by a local artist influenced by Niclaes Gerhaert. The wooden lid, similar in shape to the spire of a bell-tower, displays at the top the baptism of Jesus and lower down the seven sacraments.

Pages 48/49
A group of figures on the lid of the baptismal font in the chapel of St. Catherine.
On the left: the sacrament of baptism.
On the right: the sacrament of marriage.
From the sixteenth century to 1945 this lid was used as a baldachin for the pulpit of Anton Pilgram, but the work is not by him. During the course of a restoration it was found to be appropriate to the baptismal font and was placed there as a lid. The reliefs are among the most important of the years around 1480.

Oratory of Maria Theresa (1740)

Portrait of Duke Rudolf IV, the Founder ▶
(Dom- und Diözesanmuseum)

One of the most significant paintings of the Dom- und Diözesanmuseum is the panel with the portrait of Duke Rudolf IV of Hapsburg. The painting, depicting one of the most important donors to the Cathedral of St. Stephen, was painted in 1365. It is considered the oldest portrait in which the figure depicted is painted in three-quarters, in contrast to the tradition, dating back to Roman numismatics, of representing the figure solely in profile.

St. Catherine on the altar of the chapel

Catherine, princess of Alexandria, patron saint of the wife of Duke Rudolf IV, Catherine of Luxembourg, and patron of the University of Vienna founded by him, converted fifty pagan philosophers to Christianity and because of her testimony of faith was tortured and decapitated. Thus we see again the wheel and the sword as some of her symbols. This sculpture is heavily influenced by the figurative tendencies of the Madonnas of the international Gothic ("soft style"); from the historical-artistic point of view it is related to the Madonna of Iglau, but could be slightly older, that is before 1400.

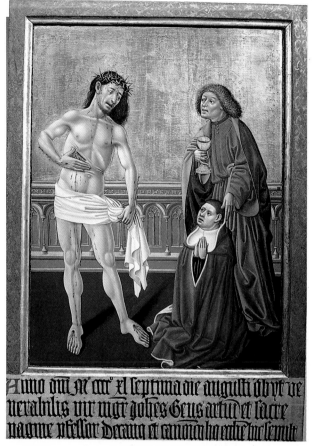

Altar-piece in memory of canon Johannes Geus
(Dom- und Diözesanmuseum)

This is the only dated altar-piece ("1440") of the Master of Albrecht, a painter who was active in Vienna and was of a level comparable to Lukas Moser, Konrad Witz and Hans Multscher; he was profoundly influenced by Flemish artists such as the Master of Flémalle and Jan van Eyck (top right). Geus was a rector at the University of Vienna. At his side is St. Thomas with Christ showing him his wounds.

Construction of the abbey church of Klosterneuburg

Detail of an alter-piece by Rueland Frueauf (collection of the abbey of Klosterneuburg), end of the fifteenth century. The painting gives us information on the working methods of Medieval architecture. We can clearly recognise hammer, chisel, ruler and mallet.

Sculptures in the Dom- und Diözesanmuseum
(the Diocesan Museum)

Original sculptures coming from the cathedral were already in the nineteenth century entering into the possession of the Kunsthistorisches Museum of Vienna due to the widescale and radical restorations; the exterior sculptures, threatened by atmospheric corrosion, have been replaced by copies. The remaining works of art in the cathedral, as well as the works of art in danger that belong to the archdiocese of Vienna, have been brought together in the Dom- und Diözesanmuseum. It contains not only a compendium of the evolution of Austrian art, but also houses masterpieces of notable importance on a European scale.

The Erlach Madonna
(Dom- und Diözesanmuseum)

This pretty Madonna from 1325, with strongly western connotations, originally comes from Erlach near Pitten in Lower Austria. It enters again into the tradition of the Madonnas that can be admired on the central pilasters of the French cathedrals of the thirteenth century. In her left hand she probably held an apple, the symbol of original sin, from which the Redeemer liberated mankind.

St. Rocho
(Dom- und Diözesanmuseum)

This is a sculpture from an altar of the cathedral from the time of Pilgram, around 1500. Rocho, patron saint of the infected, between the end of the thirteenth century and the beginning of the fourteenth, came to Italy as a pilgrim and cured many plague victims. He too contracted the plague (as indicated from the inflammation on his right leg), but succeeded in recovering.
The sculpture of St. Rocho is part of the old late-Gothic arrangement of the cathedral of St. Stephen, which included in all 48 medieval altars.

Deposition from the cross
(Dom- und Diözesanmuseum)

A sculptural group in polychromatic wood, which was probably positioned on the jubé (half-way between the choir and the nave) and dates from around 1340. The literary matrix of the iconography is the mystical dialogue of Anselm of Canterbury, in which in a dream he asked the Madonna what she had felt during the passion of Christ. In the sculptural creativity of this group we see the stylistic links with France and Tuscany.

59 KREUZABNAHME
um 1340

Engraved altar of Antwerp
(Dom- und Diözesanmuseum)

This altar was constructed in an era in which the engraved altars of Antwerp — of high artistic quality, but unoriginal from a compositional point of view — were not yet quite mass-produced. Initially acquired by the Emperor Francis Joseph for Ambras castle in Tyrol, this altar, coming originally from Pfalzel near Trier, for a century was part of the furbishing of the Votivkirche of Vienna and was then transferred, in order to be preserved better, to the Dom- und Diözesanmuseum. It is by far the most famous of these engraved Flemish altars.

Constructed in 1460, for its painted colouring (which is still almost completely intact) and for its figurative style it is the sculptural equivalent of van Eyck's early style.

The scenes depicted proceed from left to right. In the left panel we see Christ carrying the cross; low in the centre the nailing to the

cross, above, the crucifixion; in the
right panel the deposition and the
mourning for the dead Jesus.
The rich painting of this altar
engraved in oak wood creates a
touching and animated ensemble.
Above: detail of Christ carrying
the cross.
Below: deposition and mourning
the dead Christ.

Mourning the dead Christ
(Dom- und Diözesanmuseum)

This polychromatic relief too was
influenced, in its chromatic
quality, by Flemish painting. We
see in its expressive character the
Dutch influence, coming by way of
the work of Niclaes Gergaert (who
built the tomb of Frederick III) in
Vienna and in Wiener Neustadt.
The wooden relief probably comes
originally from a late-Gothic
panelled altar of south-east
Lower Austria. To the left o
Mary is Joseph of Arimathea who
asks of Pilate to allow him bury
the body of Jesus in a tomb
excavated from the rocks. Beside
him is the youngest apostle, John
the Evangelist. On the right hand
side there are three female figures
with profoundly touching
expressions. Beside Mary there is
a delicate, virginal figure with
long, flowing hair; next, with a
vase of ointment, is Mary
Magdelen; on her right is a figure
with face almost completely
hidden, yet whose suffering
is expressed with great
intensity.

Tabernacle
(Dom- und Diözesanmuseum)

This tabernacle, an early Baroque work of Palermo, was located at one time on an altar of the cathedral. Partially inlaid coloured marble has been used in its construction. The capitals and bases of the columns are of bronze.

Altar of Ober St. Veit
(Dom- und Diözesanmuseum)

The name comes from the altar's previous location in the castle of Ober St. Veit (now Vienna XIII). When open it has scenes from the Passion: Christ carrying the cross, the crucifixion, and, on the right panel, the resurrection. First commissioned to Albrecht Dürer, it is stylistically linked to many of his sketches. Hans Schäufelein, a pupil of Dürer's, built the altar, bringing together more than one design. It is the most significant crucifixion altar of early sixteenth century German painting.

Vestments

From left to right: chasuble from the Breuner vestment (1647), cope of the vestment of Eleanor (1697), Marian chasuble (end of seventeenth century), Papal chasuble (about 1740). Among the vestments used for the great liturgical festivities that have survived almost completely intact, two stand out as the most important in the historical property of the cathedral's sacresty: the "Breuner vestment" of 1647 (created for the consecration of the main, proto-Baroque altar, which took its name from the then bishop Philip count of Breuner), with its deep red

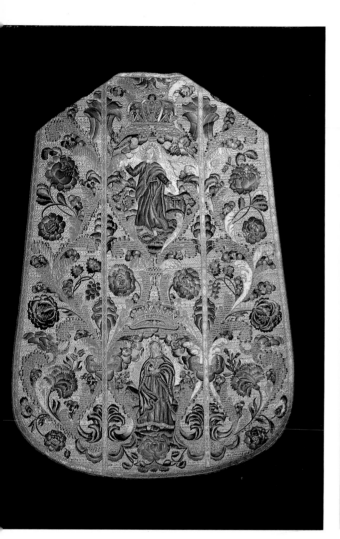

base and shapely gold embroidery that recalls the
Grotesque in form, and the "vestment of Eleanor",
created in 1697 when the miraculous image of Maria
Pötsch was transferred from the Hungarian village of
Pocs by the empress Eleanor; it has leaf decorations,
splendidly coloured ribbons and mosaic effect
embroidery.

The "Marian chasuble" stems from the late
seventeenth century, with its intense and varied
colours, its rich floral decoration and luminous effect
embroidery, while the "Papal chasuble" was donated
by Pope Pious VI on the occasion of his visit to the
cathedral of St. Stephen in 1782.

It is a work that dates from the years around 1740.

◄ Sculptures of the founders from the southern tower

(Kunsthistorisches Museum, Vienna)

These notable monumental sculptures of larger-than-life proportions, sculpted around 1360/65, are authentic expressions of the high international level reached in the figurative arts of Vienna during the fourteenth and fifteenth centuries, to be explained chiefly by the activity of the cathedral's construction. The statue of Duke Albrecht II (on the left), father of Rudolf IV is a masterpiece of particular importance both for the individuality of the pose and for the remarkably portait-like sculpting of the face. The emperor Charles IV (right), father of Rudolf IV's wife Catherine of Luxembourg, is turning towards someone with an expression and a spontaneous movement of the body that breaks away from any statuesque rigidity.

Sculptures of the cathedral

(Kunsthistorisches Museum, Vienna)

Above: a young king from an Adoration of the Magi (1390 circa). Bottom left: the Madonna with the child Jesus and Saint Anne, from 1320 (the bust of Mary is from 1360), which perhaps was used again in the series of sculptures above the atrium of the southern tower. Saint Paul from the atrium of the southern tower, about 1380 (bottom right).